ARTIST TRANSCRIPTIONS PIANO

the Gonzalo Rubalcaba collection

ISBN 0-634-05151-2

HAL•LEONARD® CORPORATION

7777 W. BLUEMOUND RD. P.O. BOX 13819 MILWAUKEE, WI 53213

Visit Hal Leonard Online at
www.halleonard.com

the Gonzalo Rubalcaba collection

contents

Bésame Mucho

(Kiss Me Much)
from *The Blessing*

Music and Spanish Words by Consuelo Velazquez
English Words by Sunny Skylar

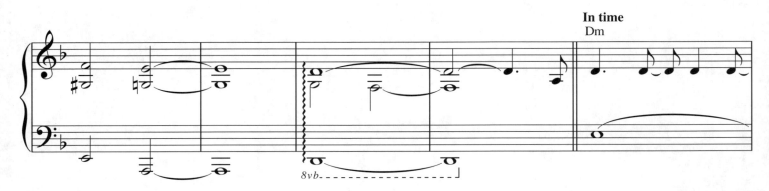

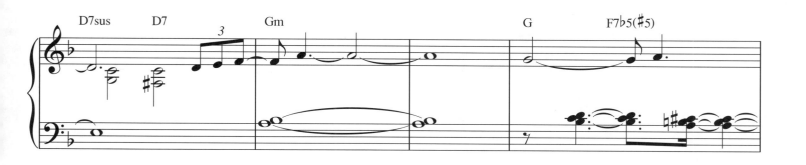

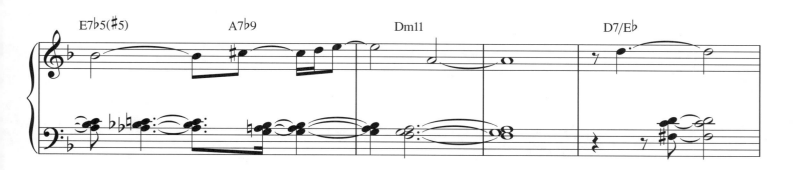

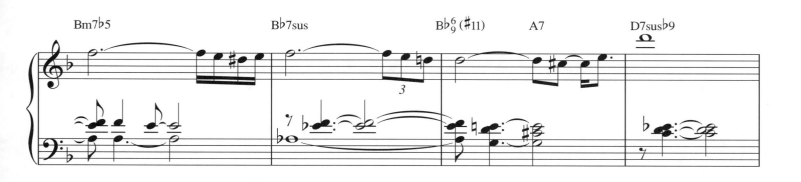

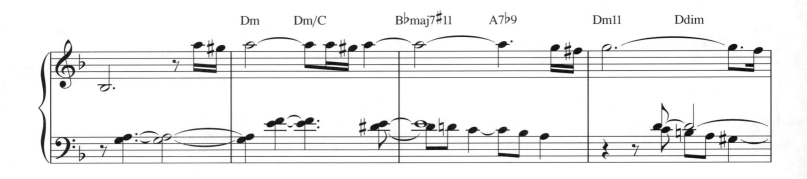

9

Donna Lee

from *Diz*

By Charlie Parker

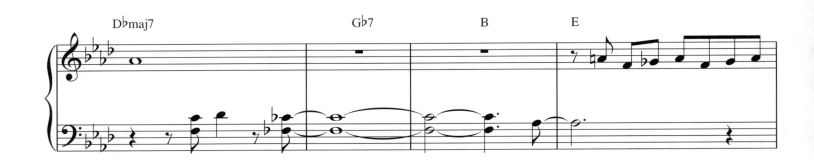

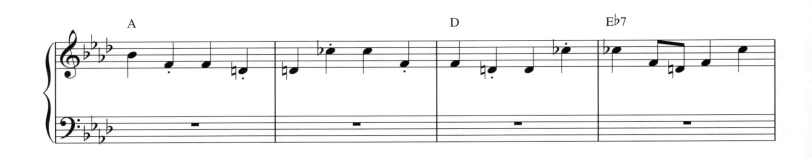

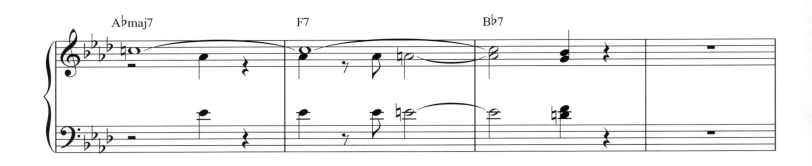

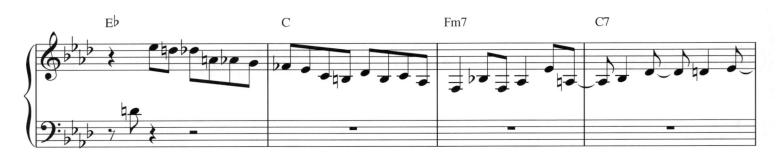

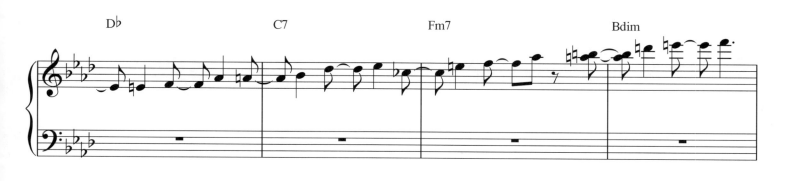

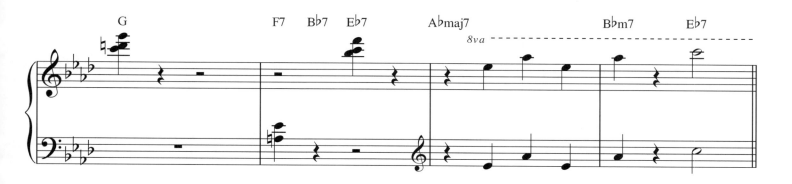

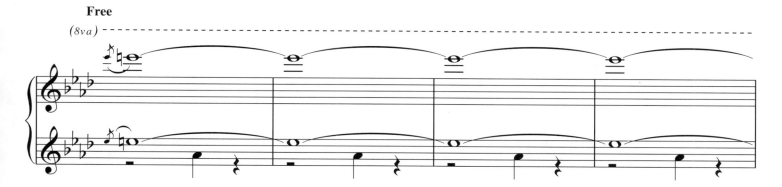

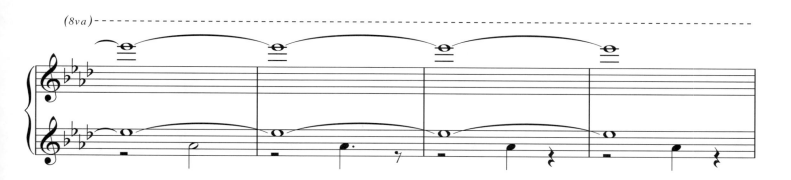

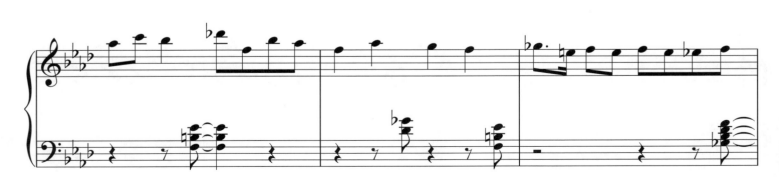

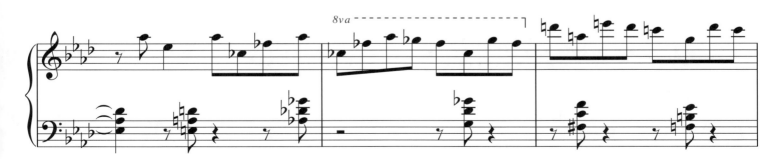

cluster

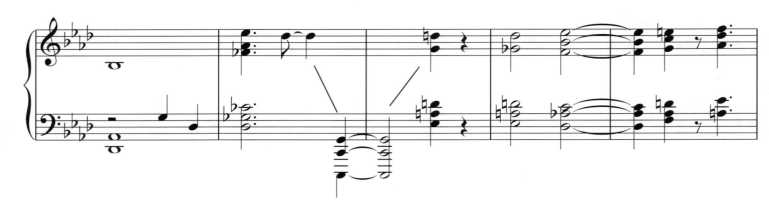

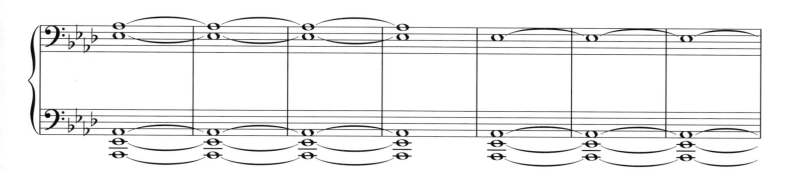

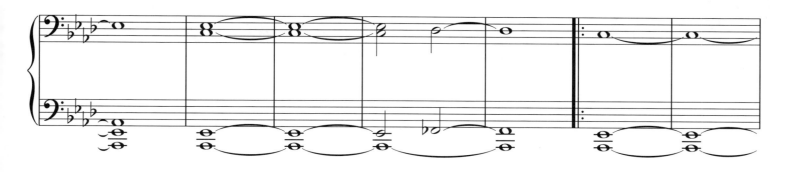

Repeat for bass ad lib.

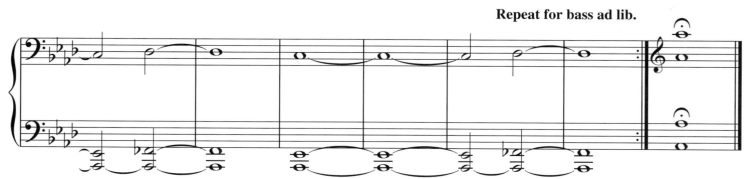

El Cadete Constitucional

from *Supernova*

By Gonzalo Rubalcaba

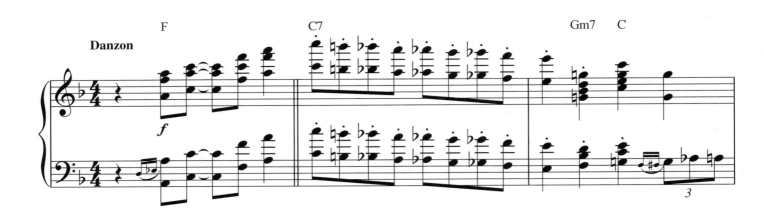

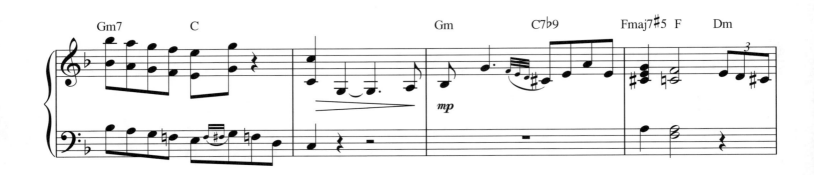

29

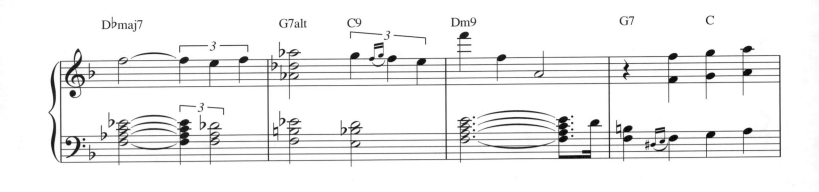

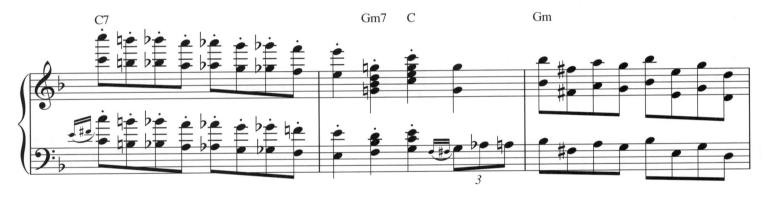

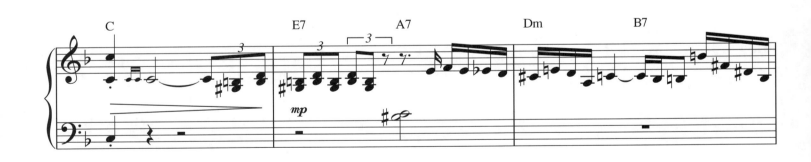

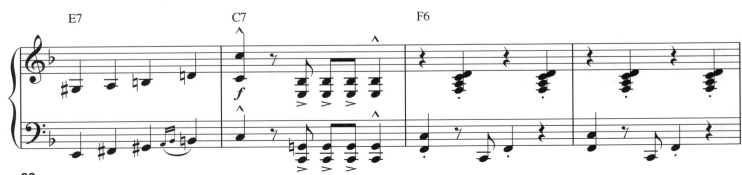

40

Prologo Comienzo
from *Discovery*
By Gonzalo Rubalcaba

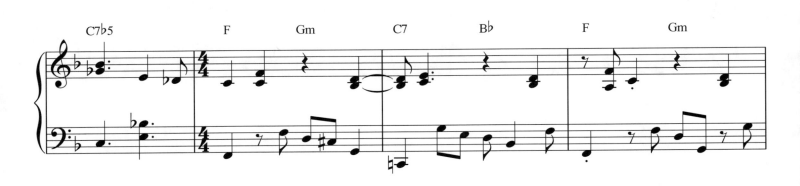

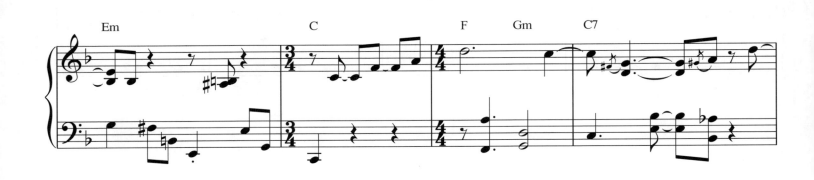

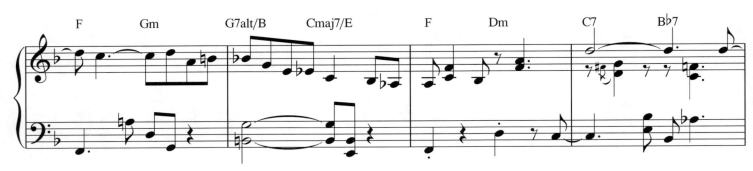

43

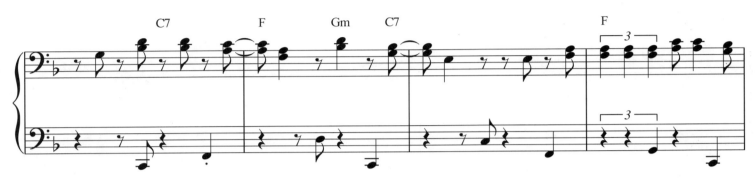

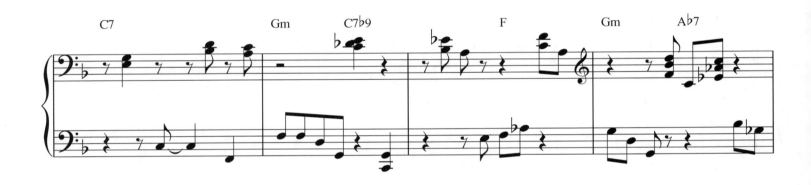

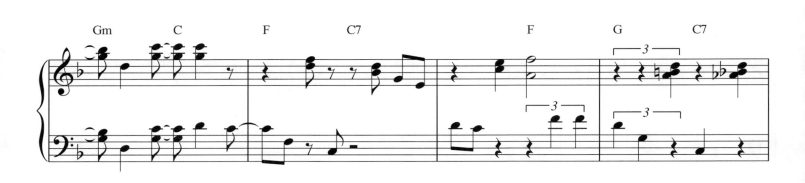

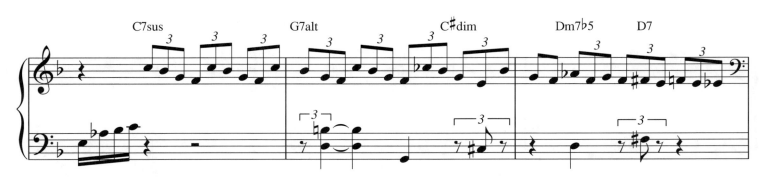

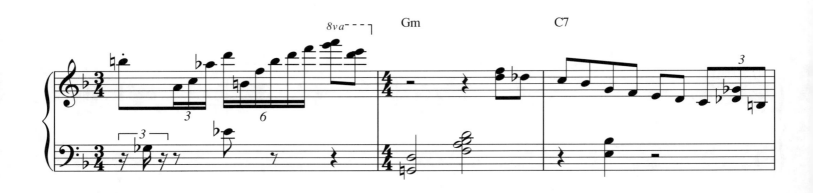

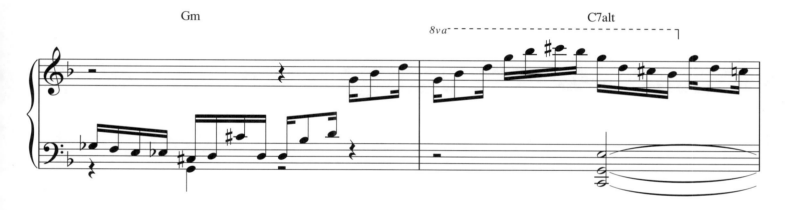

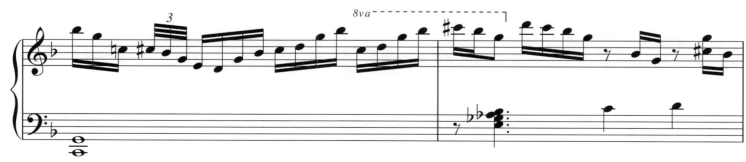

Imagine

from *Images-Live at Mt. Fuji*

Words and Music by John Lennon

Ballad, half-time feel

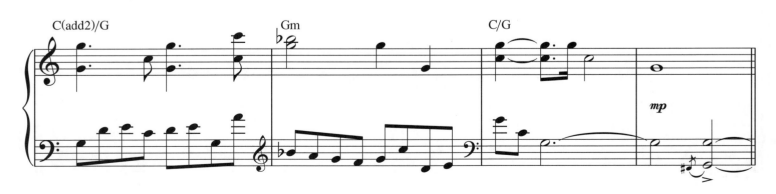

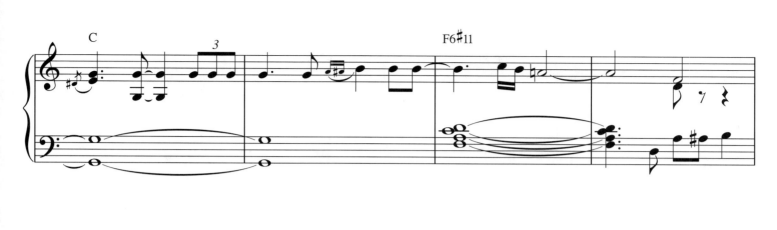

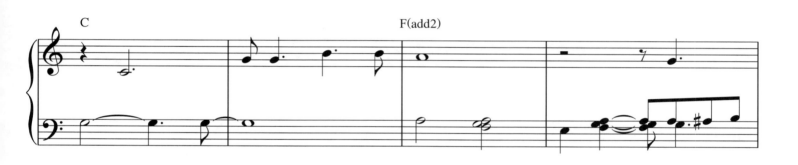

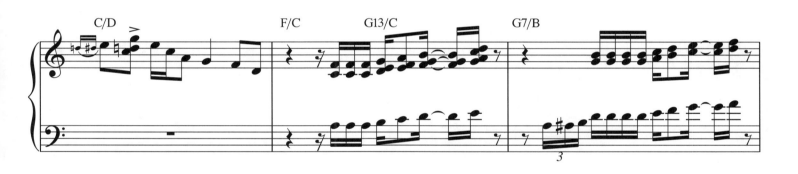

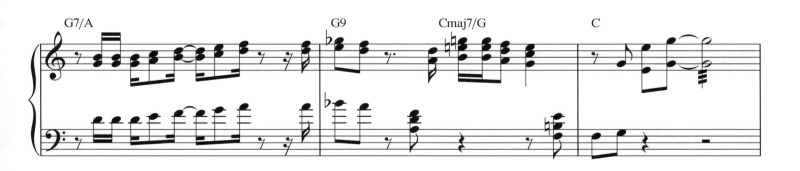

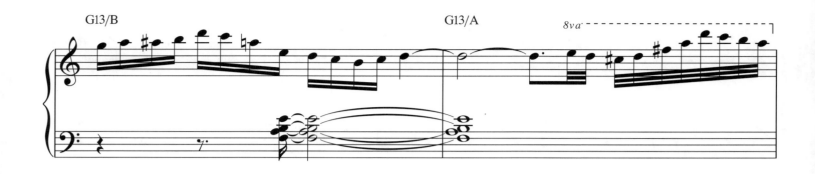

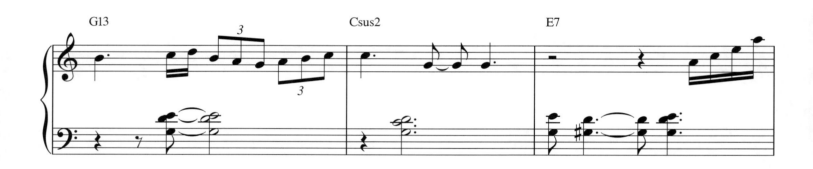

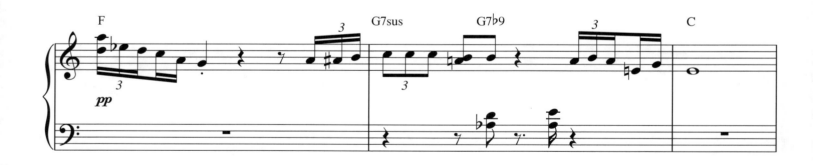

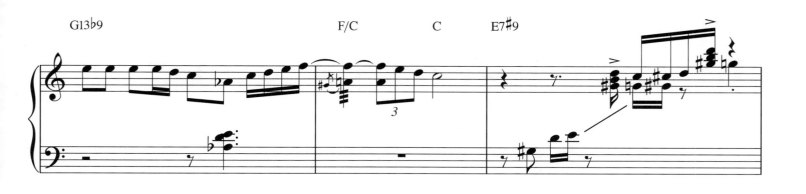

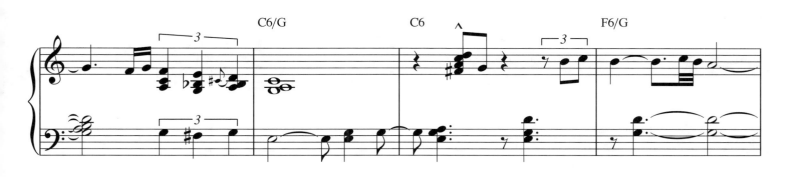

Mima

from *The Blessing*

By Gonzalo Rubalcaba

With feeling

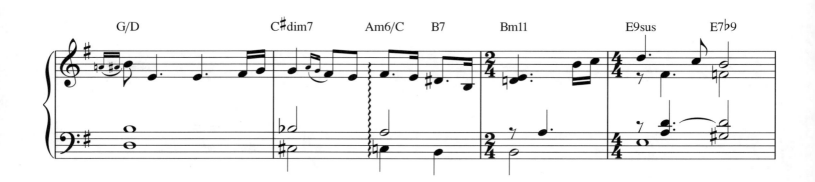

73

Otra Mirada

(Another View)
from *Supernova*
By Gonzalo Rubalcaba

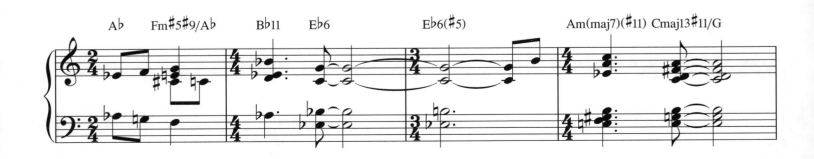

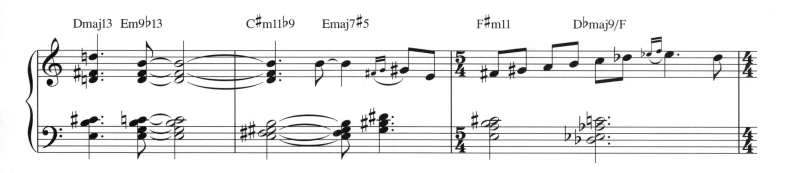

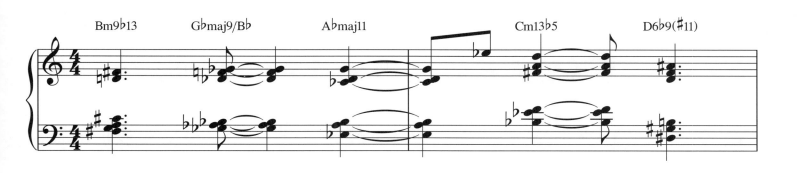

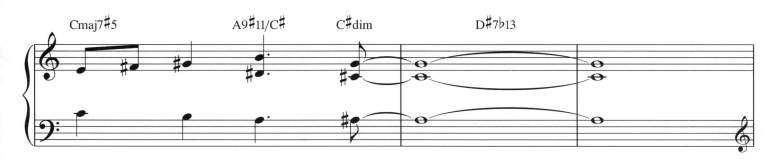

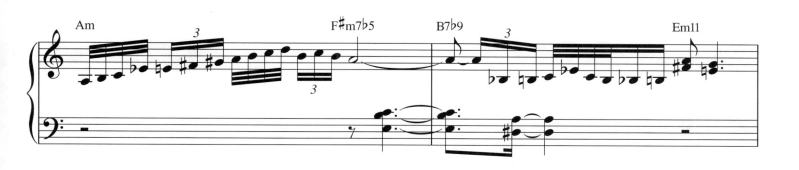

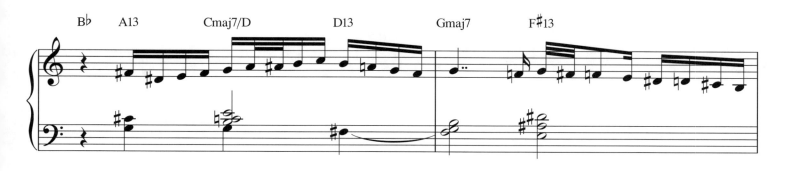

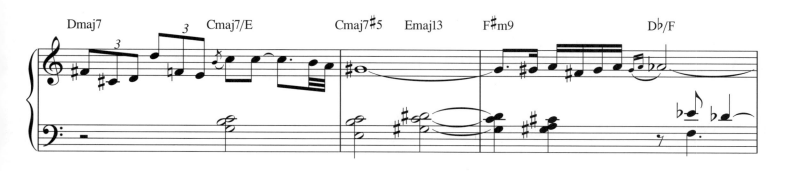

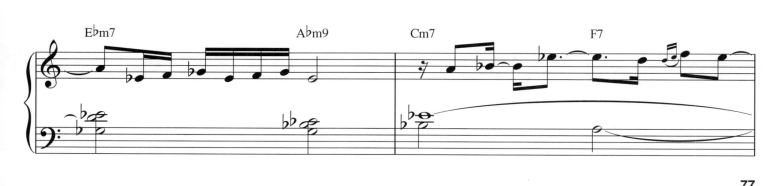

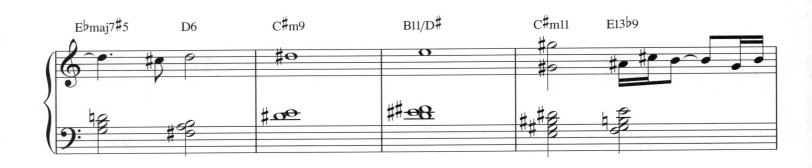

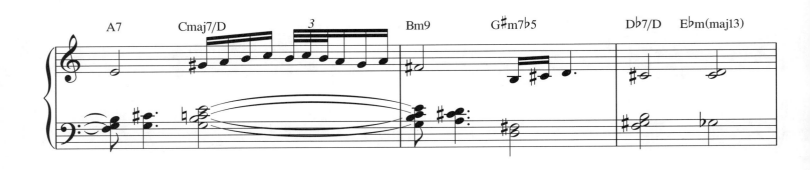

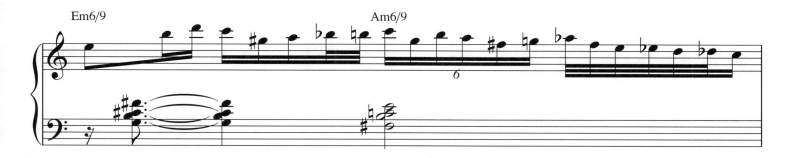

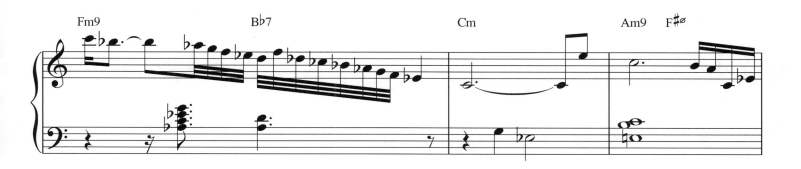

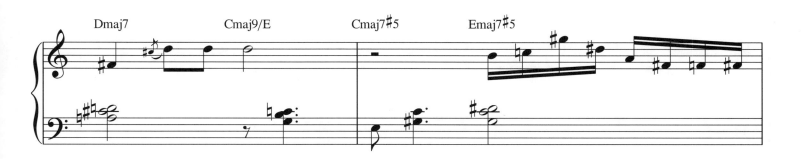

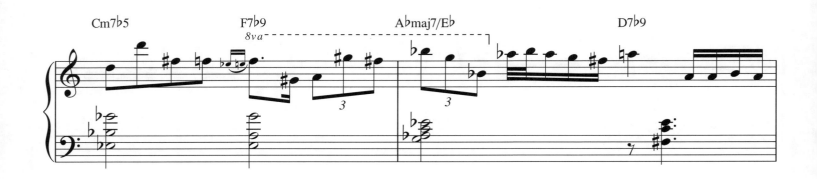

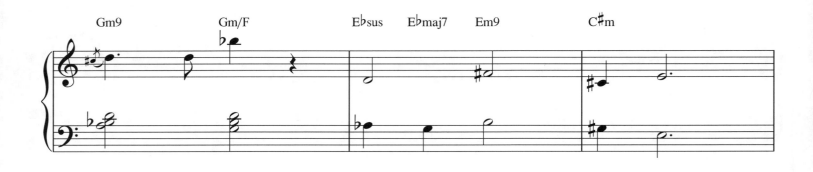

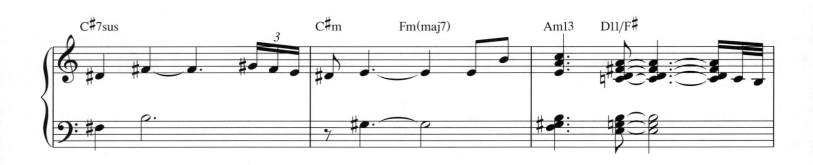

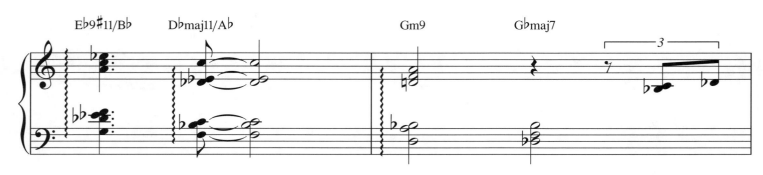

Supernova 1

from *Supernova*
By Gonzalo Rubalcaba

Latin Fusion ♩ = 80-86

* *Use sostenuto pedal for this chord.*

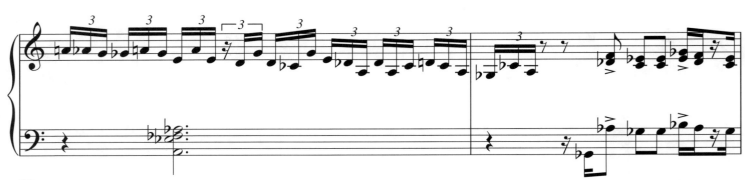

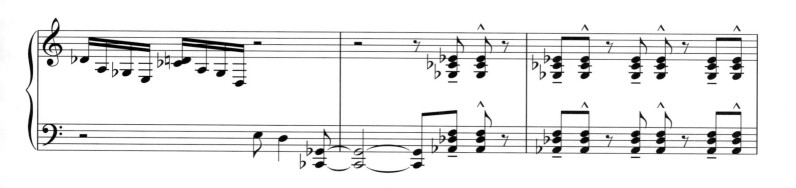

Supernova 2

from *Supernova*

By Gonzalo Rubalcaba

Latin Fusion ♩ = 120

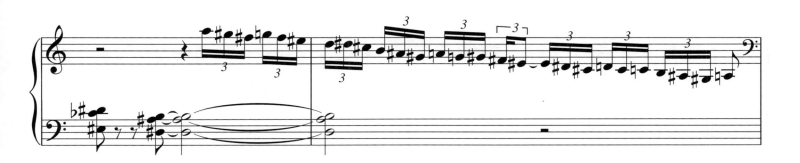

Woodyn' You

from *Diz*

By Dizzy Gillespie

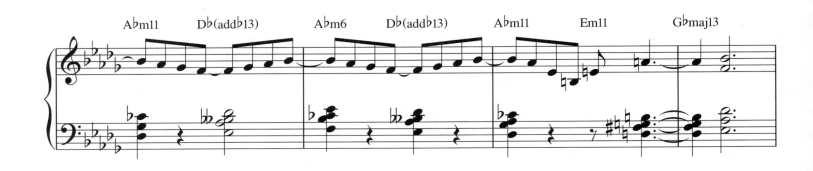

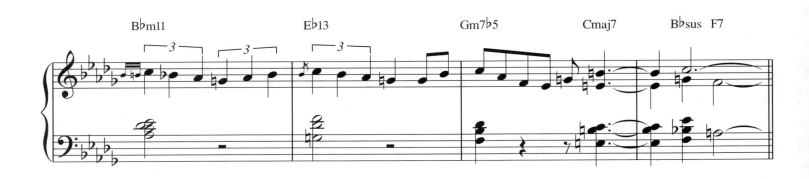

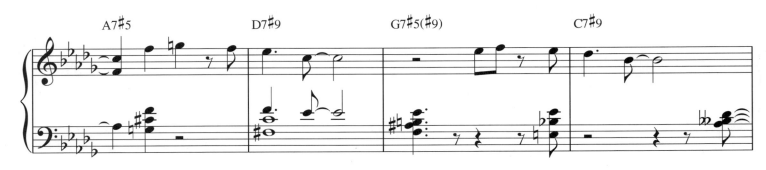

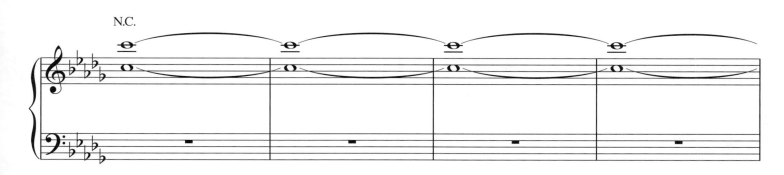

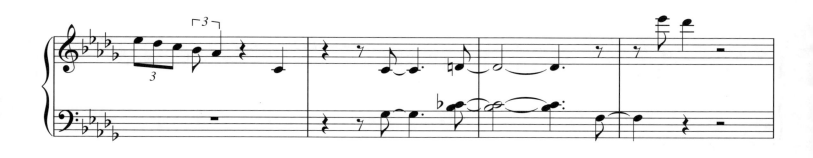

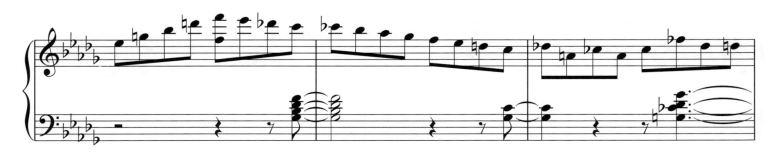

120

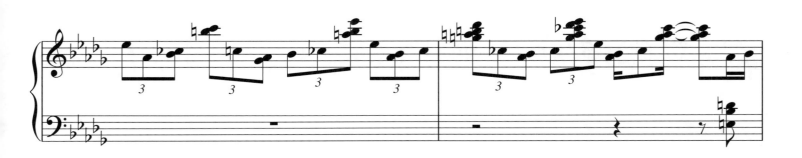

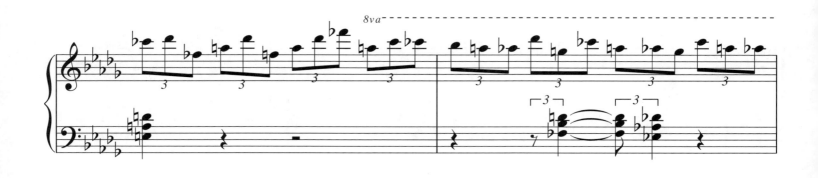

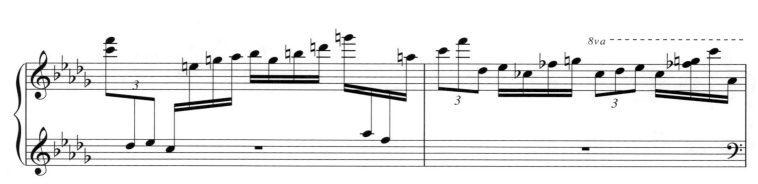

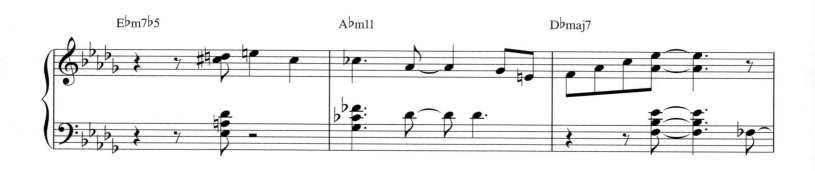

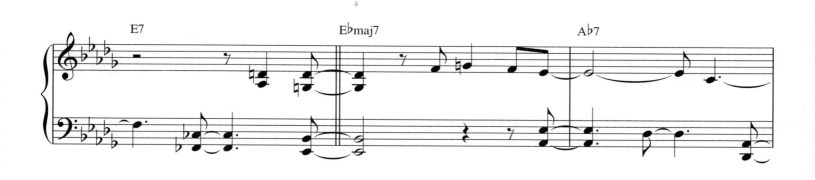

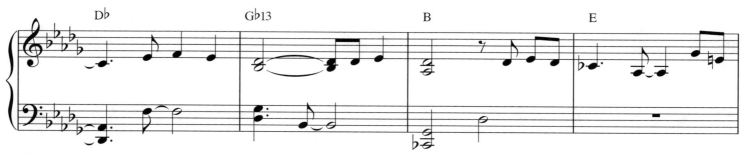

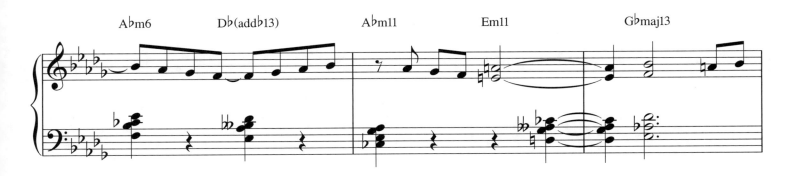

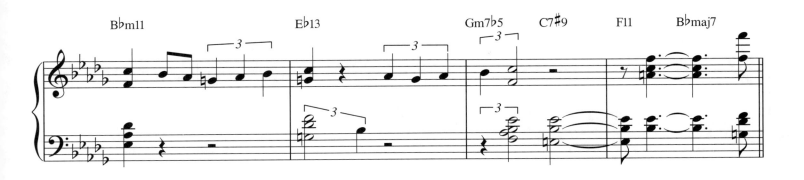

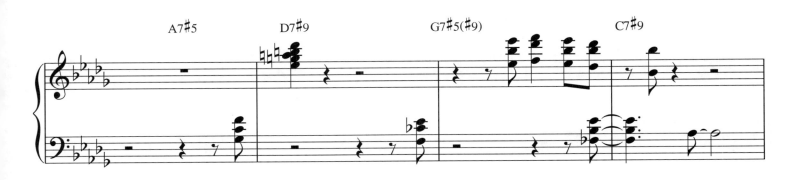

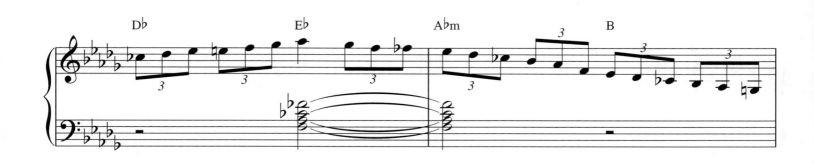

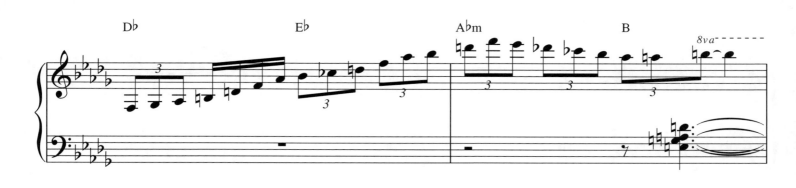

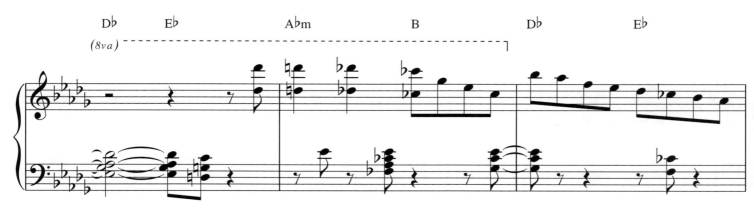

Repeat ad lib. and Fade